FROM THE YELLOW HOUSE AND ON

SOJOURNER DAVIDSON

FROM THE YELLOW HOUSE AND ON

SOJOURNER
DAVIDSON

ISBN: 979-8-218-21022-9

Library of Congress Control Number: 2023908949

Cover Art by Kate Mitchell
Edited by Read Davidson
Layout Design by Tell Tell Poetry
Photography by Dylan Parsons

First Edition

Printed by Lulu Press, Inc. in the USA.

Tending Verses, LLC
Virginia Beach, VA
Fairfax, VA

tendingverses.com

ACKNOWLEDGMENTS

Thanks to my readers and editors, Hannah Johnson, Lorren Lemmons, Read Davidson, and Kim Jackson Davidson for providing me with essential feedback and support on my manuscript. Thank you to Carmen McFarlin, your photography made the beautiful cover art of Kate Mitchell possible. Thank you to Kate Mitchell for providing me with excellent cover art (people do judge books by their covers). Thank you to Dylan Parsons at Dylan Parsons Photography for my stellar headshot. Thank you to Joy Sullivan and all my friends in the Sustenance writing group for cheering me on and giving me courage to chase this wild dream. Thanks to all of my friends and family and everyone who financially supported this endeavor. Lastly, thank you to the team at Tell Tell Poetry for formatting and designing my book.

CONTENTS

That Tree In My Town   1

The Wellington Rescue   2

In The Swamp Town   4

Dyslexia   6

Peanut Butter Popcorn   7

Absence   9

Home   10

Siblings   11

Read   12

Damn College Kids   13

Color These Scribbles   14

Love Is A Wooden Spoon   15

Crowded By You   16

From A Spill   17

[   ]   18

The Last Thanksgiving With You Was The Worst   19

Unraveling Daughter   20

Not Your Mountain Son   21

Cooking Omelettes   22

Learning To Become Invisible   23

Thanks Dad   24

Fucking Stains   25

Boys   26

Nigg@r B!tch   27

There Were Lights   28

Men Who Creep   30

During The Night   31

Asexual Student   32

Never Again   33

En Pointe   35

(Not Again)   36

Code Switch   37

Volleyball   38

When I Needed You   39

Berry Cobbler   40

Filler Beads   41

Snow Days   42

A Box Without Holes   43

In Biology Lab   44

Fried Green Tomatoes With Depression   45

Lavender Oil   46

You Will Need A Tissue   47

To Meeko Israel   48

Cat Tongue   49

What You're Good For   50

Tending Fires   51

In The Arbor   52

Goodbye   53

THAT TREE IN MY TOWN

That tree in my town
Makes a canopy
A home to sit in the lit night
On benches made by human
Hands
Striping away at beauty
To build a museum around
That tree

I feel transported
Someplace only me and this tree exist
I can almost hear it's roots
I let it's bark alone
Like a masterpiece
I only look
Until a noisy stranger comes

THE WELLINGTON RESCUE

Our town is famous for many things: Home to the first college to accept women and black people, 99th stop on the Underground Railroad and remember; the Wellington rescue.

1856: John Price breaks his chains, makes his way to the swampy town of Oberlin Ohio.

September 1858: A gentleman pays an unexpected visit. Mr. Price is captured under the pretense of a job offer; the 1850 Fugitive Slave Law kicks in the door.

Price is transported to the meanest depths of the heart of America: Wellington. From Wellington word gets back to this "liberal haven," Oberlin.

Langston (not Langston Hughes, wrong place, wrong race, wrong period), Charles Langston attempted a legal fight; guess how well that went?

Unwilling to back down, Langston said, fuck it; let's break some laws.

Langston and other abolitionists comrades stormed the tower (okay, hotel) Price was being held at and built him a portal to Canada.

Ugh, breaking laws (no matter how unjust) comes with consequences; Langston and a crowd of his companions were arrested for violating the Fugitive Slave Law.

The story goes on: people rallied around these men and the cause they held, wrote damning words and spoke soaring speeches that tugged on the ribbons of hearts.

These words rocked law into action; the kidnappers were charged and arrested (for a while).

By July 1859: every participant in Price's freedom saw their own again.

IN THE SWAMP TOWN

I lived in a swamp town
In a cracked yellow house
With birds in the roof
And squirrels in the walls
Ponds used to gather in the fall

I once saw a duck in my backyard
Spring summer groundhogs
On the right side
On all sides it was a weird wild world
It was beautiful but broken

It was metal on the left
When she ripped into the yellow house
Well it wasn't even a home
When she left, she left her eyes
And the yellow house was never really
My home
Again

A few years down the line
We had to leave
We couldn't save the yellow house
It couldn't care for us
So we found something blue
We moved and we moved
And I left the swamp town
I moved around

Now I'm back in the swamp town
In something blue
We see deer in the back and birds
In the trees
In the bushes there are chipmunks

We have a dog and a cat
They are so funny together
On all sides it's a weird wild world
Beautiful and broken

DYSLEXIA

You thought pepper on eggs was gross
I thought ketchup on eggs was weird
I didn't know how to spell happy
You thought that was funny
I told you I have a superpower
You told me to tell no one

PEANUT BUTTER POPCORN

I once saw a duck
In the pond
We sometimes had
In our swampy backyard

I planted popcorn seeds
And watched them not grow

We swung so high
We twisted
And slid down the slide filled with leaves

My friend and I
We ate peanut butter on popcorn

She
Ate peanut butter on everything
Even salami

We were
So weird
We both liked broccoli

We were friends because I asked her to be
We played with Bratz not Barbies

I mostly drew
I couldn't
Read

Guess what
I could write
Roads away

My friend disappears
For the answer

Still
so far away when I return
She still eats peanut butter in salami
But we've changed too much

ABSENCE

I remember swinging
Towards a sunset
And losing sight of the world

HOME

When I was young
Home was hard to find

I went searching
In pencil boxes
I found home
In a picture
I found home
In the colors

I grew out of
A yellow house
And into a home
I could take anywhere
With me

SIBLINGS

My sibling
Has snickering classmates
Ones who speak it to their back
Say it to their face
There is always the ring leader
I whisper, "make some tea"
I push a teabag into their hand
At the next chance
There are tea leaves all up in
Silky blond hair
There is tea between siblings
Clinking cups
Drinking the white girl tears
Over laughter
To soothe the blues
Make a friend out of an enemy too

READ

You hide under your hoodie
Forget your nose in books
Walk while reading
Study the pages
Better than the world?
I wonder what your face looks like
I haven't seen it in a while
What does your world look like?
I'd like to wander through sometime

DAMN COLLEGE KIDS

As a child
I listened
To the college kids
Scream and giggle
Drunkenly
Into a school night
I'd wake up to beer
Cans and Solo cups
Littered on the front yard
The party
Seemed
To never end
In the house next door
The night was full of whoops and hollers
Calls to the landlord
And shouting out windows
The night
Did not
Bring rest

COLOR THESE SCRIBBLES

I've always wanted to tell stories
There were only those I could draw for awhile
I was fastidious with my coloring pages
And drawings
As a child
Reading was staring at marks
My diaries were scribbles
Of embarrassment
I lived in images
I imagined the stories to go with them
When the images did not appear
There was no way to pretend
The color in me muted
I walked in little deaths

LOVE IS A WOODEN SPOON

The dishwasher doesn't work
The bathroom floor is sinking in
Squirrels play in the walls
(Scratch-scratch, skitter-skitter)
The house has become more of a mess
Since you came
And tried to clean it up

I am afraid of the dark
But I am more scared of the sound you make
Climbing the stairs
With your weighty breath

Ready to come tell me love is a wooden spoon
Love is harsh words
Slapped from the lungs
Love is pulling me out of whatever safety
I try to create
From you

CROWDED BY YOU

All the women crowd me
And take away my breath
I realize it is just my grandmother

FROM A SPILL

Spilled liquid makes
Fists of words
Makes a sister split
Takes her away
For little bits
Makes me wonder if she'll get her twirl back
They don't understand
Some of that twirl is her
She heals from that trespass
And recovers her jazz
Makes music that flings fists away
And spills into purposeful plays

[   ]

I still remember your smell
Sweaty baby No. 5 steamed up your room
You weren't anything like a baby when you barreled through our home
Uprooted bushes
Cleaned dishes in a tub of their own murk
Brought your teaching to my ears
Made me run from words
Brought your teaching to my body
Until you closed yourself in your room
And steamed it up for a few days
Until you were ready to try your teaching again

THE LAST THANKSGIVING WITH YOU WAS THE WORST

I was tied to my seat in a room with you
You yelled at us for not doing things your way
And I broke out of my ties and reminded you
Thanksgiving was about giving thanks
(this is before I learned the true Thanksgiving story, a story to end in mourning)
Then—"brat"
You scattered into the kitchen
Flung the fridge open
And swung from the ceiling with your voice
I left
I lay in my bed until he came up (afraid it was you creaking up the steps)
My father dismissed your behavior
And told me to go down and help with the dishes
I helped, screaming from my lungs
On the inside
You watched with your preyful eyes

UNRAVELING DAUGHTER

A daughter unravels some of her clothes
To thread the holes in her father
She sweeps the crumbs he has left
And goes to bed
A little less whole than the day before

NOT YOUR MOUNTAIN SON

The divine will not wait
For you to climb a mountain
When you return
You may not recognize
Who they have become

While you searched
For a mountain son
You lost more than a mountain

The divine do not wait
For fathers looking
For mountain sons
You don't recognize the divine
You see gestalt

COOKING OMELETTES

I learned to cook by watching my father
He made omelettes for breakfast
I watched him whisk
Chop
Pour
Fry
And flip
Our relationship involved a lot of pour and flip
I'd pour he'd flip
A tiresome trick
Not to be used outside of the kitchen
This sizzle was not satisfying
There was also some chopping
"I wish I had a son"
"You're a girly girl"
Pour
"I like . . ."
tease
You hurt me
that's not my fault!
Pour
Flip
Pour
Flip
Pour
Flip
I am learning not to make omelettes of my relationships

LEARNING TO BECOME INVISIBLE

I had your picture on my dresser
Looked at it every night
Until it became the only way I could see your face

THANKS DAD

My dad was really into MMA
On our walks he would sometimes randomly break out a high kick
He also taught me some moves
Moves I had to use on you
When you wrapped around me like a snake
And poisoned my love for fashion

FUCKING STAINS

Someone stained
BITCH and HO
Into the sidewalk of my school
Even the rain wouldn't wash it away
For a year
I walked to and from school
With my head bent to the ground reading those words

I wish I could go back and lift my head
Tell myself to walk towards the world
With confidence
Leave the stains to bleach away
In the sun

BOYS

Boys loved to touch
Ever since grade school
I was their toy

I became a stick
A twig
But they were rabid dogs
They bit
Left bloody tooth marks
In my sovereignty

I only turned in toward myself
But a circle is a target

I made my voice a weapon
And I was a bitch

I guess being made of bark
Was no protection

I learned eventually
I could never cure
A rabid man

NIGG@R B!TCH

The music swarms me
My body becomes a statue
To disappear from the words
I go out of my character
Tell you to turn down the music
That makes me want to do a magic act
You do and then you don't
It's all a game to you
So I go back to performing statue
And hum a song that doesn't swarm
This body

THERE WERE LIGHTS

And jazz
Ticketed pies
An art walk
I helped set up
All the best of
High school art
Priced low and big

You helped me
Carry a piece of art
Too big for my arms
And I thought it was
Something else
But you were an Asshole
Who told racist jokes
Thought calling a Jewish girl (or any girl)
A feminazi was acceptable
Apparently
Affirmative action is prejudice
Because your aunt
Didn't earn a job
In South Africa

I didn't know an Asshole
Could also be helpful
Like minisculely
Sometimes
Not really that much
But enough
When your self-confidence is so low

Illumination

MEN WHO CREEP

He was a creep
Admiring girls dance on the
Chemistry table at the front of the room
Making a lesson out of Beyonce's body
Commenting on the width of their
shoulder straps
The length of their dresses
Sending them to the office
Cause self-expression is a crime
And your wandering eyes
They are just nature science

DURING THE NIGHT

The trees outside my window
Had eyes
I dressed so timidly in my room
Until I decided
If the trees look at me
I will let my body stare at them

ASEXUAL STUDENT

Only plants are asexual
Says my natural sciences teacher

So I don't exist?
Or maybe I am
A purple tulip

P.S.

What about starfish, which split in half, regenerating into two?
Whiptail lizards?
Komodo dragons?
Hydra who bud off into others?

NEVER AGAIN

Do you remember
When I'd come to your home
We'd sleep on the floor
It was always cold
But I was glad to be near to you
Do you remember all the games we played
All the time we spent
But there was always something
Wrong with me
And you were perfect
I was yours
In a very bad way
But I loved you
Even in your worst ways
Remember when we built that dollhouse
And played with handmade dolls
We made them lovers
But that was only once
Your touch was always punishment
All sacrifices mine
I think you hated me
But I loved you in return
When everything was wrong
You saw me as a fly
We were on and off
And I was always the one more invested
It was too long
For me to get over you
As a friend

I think you were really my first love
Somehow
I still wonder about you
I do hope we've both changed
I do want you to be happy
And never want to feel the way I did
With you again

EN POINTE

You put on your ballet shoes
And dance on my heart
Till your feet are broken
And my chest is purple

(NOT AGAIN)

I sometimes dream of you
Wonder what it would be like
If we were still together

CODE SWITCH

I had to leave my home
To learn to turn marks into meaning
I went to the blue panther
With little color in its mouth
But learned the language still
I lived in a neighborhood dark
With color
And vibrant with community
Mouths opened wide
People sat out on porch steps
Making their lives a scene
Life was public
And cluttered
Unlike the huge, sparsely decorated
Houses of my classmates
My neighborhood had character
My friend's house had brightly colored walls
And a floral mural up the stairs
Houses went on a slope
We made pepper poppers
And sour cream cookies
But there was also drama
In every day you and I
Spent together
Beauty in making something good with a friend
But also tears

VOLLEYBALL

I was so terrible
At the game
They called me the determinator
The one who tries to make winter into spring
But always manages an April snow
The one who misses the setup or just nearly
The one who practices the most
But still falters
At the end
I was so good at being terrible
They gave me a name

WHEN I NEEDED YOU

It was a school night
I was was so tired when I asked that we go home
You wanted to watch the super bowl or rose bowl
You dumped me at a friend's home and went back to your game
Waiting to sleep in my own bed I played some
Dance Dance Revolution (a game I'm really bad at)
At my friends request
We beaded jewelry with one of our adult friends
I beaded my anger and my tiredness onto thin wires
Ticking away like the seconds hand on the clock
I was impatient for sleep
Impatient to be seen
As the child that needed you
Though you continued to teach me not to

BERRY COBBLER

We make a cobbler
In your tiny
One-room apartment
The colors are beautifully rich
We cut butter into flour
And make that room
Smell like favored fruits
And sugar
Maybe Cinnamon
Too
You make my life richer
Add a sweetening spice
You are a favored friend
Someone
I'll always
Find beautiful
In her warmth

FILLER BEADS

We used to bead together
String our words on bendy wire cords
Crimp on clasps
Twist ourselves together
Make a mess of picking up those tiny filler beads
While the rest was calm
I was in a circle with you
We could also string silence
Make the quiet our friend
Let the string take on our feelings
All the ones that are too hard to name
I miss those days of beading with you
Making something come together
While everything else fell apart
And we sat in silence
Putting prayers on strings

SNOW DAYS

Nothing feels like winter
Yet it is February
If I close my eyes sometimes I can image
The snow storm I grew up in
Feel the red in my face
And the choke of cold wind
I remember days when school was canceled
For too much snow or too much cold
But the real chill lay in the fluorescently
Lit halls
Of a musty middle school
In northeast Ohio
I was happy to hide away
In my creaky century home
With newspaper insulation
Happy to miss lonely in a squeeze of bodies
Always judging
Always pretending knowledge
Always cheating
As I go along
Silence on my tongue
Fire in the back of my mouth
Reflecting through my eyes
Burning a hole

A BOX WITHOUT HOLES

As a teenager
I buried myself in novels
Tucked myself between the pages
Of sketchbooks
I tried to paint my pain away
I spent lots of time thinking
In a dark room
I would sit sometimes
And long for death
Wish it with my eyes shut tight
Or staring into nothingness
I was afraid of death
I lived in a box with no holes
Trying to breathe
Forget it
My depression told my anxiety
Who needs breath
In a fiery lake
My anxiety is what keeps me
Hanging on to life
Warns me to be terrified of death
Losing my breath
Burning myself outside my imagination
Makes depression my reality
Imagination drills holes in a box
Releases breath
Lets the air flow in
Oxygen
Ahhhhh

IN BIOLOGY LAB

I raise my arms
Let my armpits breathe
Show the world
The hair between
My arms
This is freedom

FRIED GREEN TOMATOES WITH DEPRESSION

Watch Fried Green Tomatoes
Cozy in your mother's bed
Laugh and cry
The world is sad, scary, and beautiful

LAVENDER OIL

When my feelings were a storm
My mother brought the calm
Rubbed lavender oil on my feet
We'd sleep side by side
And I would be at peace

YOU WILL NEED A TISSUE

I know the definition of love
One night I sneezed in my mother's hair
Not a little *ah-chooo*
But a great big snotty sneeze
With tears streaming down my face

I was tired of the coming and going
Devastated at having to leave again
So watermelon drops fell from my face
And I sounded like a hurt dog
My mother scooped me in her arms

And there it came
A great big snotty sneeze
Mixed with tears
Right in her curly dark hair

And she didn't even flinch
We looked at each other
And laughed
My tears disappeared

And here's a tissue

TO MEEKO ISRAEL

I miss you
Your words
Your songs
Your clever tongue
And poems
Your love
So warm
Through your pain
You spoke clever songs
You laughed
And gave love
You did not hide
Or follow
But the spirit
In your soul
And the spirit of God
You inspired me
Like a rainbow
We both own the rainbow
I hope you left knowing that
God(s) and Gays
You and Me
Our rainbow
And nobodies
But you were somebody to me
I would like to hear your words now
See a rainbow

CAT TONGUE

Every summer
We chalk the sidewalks
Downtown
Coming home chalk—all over me
You lap it off of my feet
With your sandpaper tongue
Like I am your kitten

WHAT YOU'RE GOOD FOR

I see your car's not in the driveway
So I walk my dog in the backyard
You are only good for the garden
I watch out the window as the birds
Pick at the seeds
In their houses
You are good for the garden
But I remember all trespasses
So I wait for your car to go
Before I walk the dog
And enjoy what you are good for

TENDING FIRES

After graduation
I did all the things I never did
Attended parties
No
That's basically it
I attended parties
Went to houses I'd never seen
Sat with people I never
Hung out with
Ate watermelon
Because it was summer
Instead of talking to anyone
I tended fires
And looked at the face
Of an old friend

IN THE ARBOR

I miss our walks
Around town
Talking about
All the uncomfortable things
All the discomfort
Of being a teen
Walking in the Arbor
Talking about sex
And depression
Me wanting to let you know
It wasn't your fault
And not saying
The right words
I wish I hadn't
Missed that walk

GOODBYE

I'm ready to leave this place that doesn't love me
Find a peace outside of this place
Look for people whose faces do not look like mine
Find a bit of power in this grace

ABOUT THE AUTHOR

Sojourner Davidson is the owner of Tending Verses, LLC, a poetry commissions business formed in 2023. They have been published in *The Greenleaf Review*, *Knee Brace Press*, *South Broadway Ghost Society*, and *Dear Future Lover: Short Poem Anthology*. Sojourner has been writing poetry for 8 years and has come to believe that great poetry is felt both emotionally and physically. Sojourner writes to enter into this space, always balancing how words play on the mind and body. Sojourner mainly focuses their writing on politics, identity, and relationships and how these aspects ping off each other. When not writing poetry they are lounging around with their dog, speaking with loved ones, or engaging in an oscillating list of hobbies. Their greatest hope is to make people feel through their writing.

www.ingramcontent.com/pod-product-compliance
Lightning Source LLC
Chambersburg PA
CBHW070013100426
42741CB00012B/3223